Prism Poetry

Refracting Life

Timothy M. Bowers

authorHOUSE®

AuthorHouse™
1663 Liberty Drive
Bloomington, IN 47403
www.authorhouse.com
Phone: 1-800-839-8640

First published by AuthorHouse   4/27/2011

ISBN: 978-1-4567-5677-2 (e)
ISBN: 978-1-4567-5289-7 (hc)
ISBN: 978-1-4567-5290-3 (sc)

Library of Congress Control Number: 2011904365

Printed in the United States of America

Thanks

First of all I want to give thanks to God for giving me the ability to write and for opening opportunities to share my thoughts. I want to thank my parents, Jerry and Demarice for their encouragement and support through this project and my brother Chris for his superb illustrations. I also want to thank my cousin Jennifer who always made time to read and review my poems whenever she got the chance. To my friends Bernadette and Ishanie, I want to thank them for their help with inspiration and for keeping me on course. Finally all my family and friends who have helped me create this book thank you so much!

Contents

Chapter 4: Diverse

Chapter 5: Faith

Chapter 1: Encouragement

O Warrior king, how heralds sing
Of mighty battles long ago
With shield and sword, you charged toward
And fell each valiant foe

Trophies gained, by enemies slain
Medals and honours abound
Legend created, never debated
Forever your name be renowned

But what years have passed, since you last
Appeared on field of battle
With steed drawn near, with silver spear
To meet the clash and rattle

For now your old, your story told
Tarnished the trophies of then
You're body weak, your fervour meek
Wishing to relive days of when

Your blade broken, now mere token
Of times when you were young
Your battered shield, unfit to wield
No exploits now be sung

So what to do, your life is through
Allow time to wash away
Remain at home, upon royal throne
Forever lost to yesterday

But you instead, dare to tread
To steel plate and hanging mail
Donning arms, to face the harms
Of swinging club and thrashing flail

With each strike, and slashing pike
Life returns to your veins
Your battle call, heard by all
The Warrior king again shall reign

Author Notes: When I wrote this poem all I saw in my mind was a picture of an old warrior sitting on a throne with sword in hand. I find this is how many of my poems are created, just seeing an image and then try to write from what I saw. They say a picture is worth a thousand words and although its cliché you would be surprised how true the statement is. I could have gone several directions when writing this but the fact that the warrior still held his sword pushed me towards a tale of renewal.

By Your Side

No matter the reason no matter the cause
Know that we are there without pause
Sending our love in the ways we know how
Hoping our gift may help in your time now

Through the hurt and through the tears
We will continue to draw near
And when unanswered questions fill your mind
Know we are praying during those trying times

During times of night, absent of light
We will be there to lend you our sight
To help you see lies some would have you believe
And ensure their evil plots will never achieve

Despite if it's now or when we have all grown
Always remember that you are not alone
Find the father and curl up into his arms
There find peace and comfort free from harm

When you look to the sky and view each star
May you be reminded we will never be far
Watching over when things are too much to bear
In those times know that we are there.

Connected

To live in this world, and miss the truth
It would be wise to spare the youth
Spare them the teachings of the blind
Spare them the confusion of our mind

Only when the scales have fallen away
Can we view the world of today
See that all is connected to each other
With strings that join one to another

From the core of one, to the core of the earth
To the core of one from a different birth
These strings unseen, yet not obscene
Connect us all by various means

Strings that become slack or taught
Through the course of life and thought
Such thin bonds with strength unknown
With the power to move muscle and bone

Because of this, you must be sure
To bond with those sound and pure
For if they choose to tread selfish halls
You will join them in the fall

Carefully examine your connections
Cut loose from those pulling in wrong directions
Be prepared to heal and mend
Frayed edges belonging to true friends

With the knowledge stored in your heart
That you're connected from the very start
Finally you will begin to understand
That if the world is like glass, we are the sand

Author Notes: This piece was inspired when I was talking with an old friend from high school and we were surprised that although we haven't seen each other in years we shared a lot of random mutual friends. That got me thinking about the idea of 6 degrees of separation; everyone can be linked to another just by 6 connected relationships. We think that the world is so vast and foreign to us but when you think of the random people you meet in your life; your span of influence is pretty shocking.

Fate

Bullet shot, Bullet dropped
Released level at same point of time
Separating faster than sound
Their lives forever intertwined

One born of explosive force
Intricate device to establish the course
The other given to natural design
To freely choose with no remorse

One speeding through horizontal plane
Diverse sights to behold and retain
The other with slow and vertical drop
Happy to live in one spot and remain

One with strong reverberating sound
To make those aware when it's around
The other silent in a world its own
Content to listen to the stories abound

Each bullet different in every way
But still their lives are intertwined
Despite how hard they may attempt
The ground they'll reach at the same time

Author notes: This is a philosophical question posed to students that the tv
show mythbusters actually tested. When I watched the episode there was no
way that I thought that the two bullets would hit the ground simultaneously
but lo and behold they did. Despite all the factors that could have affected the
results not one of them made a difference.

Island

I am an island
Alone
Floating on the waters of life

Carried by the current
Unknown
Is my destination

I scream at the ocean
Hoping
For the faintest response

But I hear none
Funny
The irony of my situation

Spending all my life
Trying
To push away those who cared

Thinking to myself
If only
I could escape the consequence

Then I could find
Surely
A bit of happiness

Living independent
Allowing
My life to commence

Now that I'm alone
Free
To do as I please

Wonder why so many
Choose
To stay with each other

No one to answer to
Surely
This is paradise

I mean isn't it weak
Needing
To rely on one another

But now that I am here
Isolated
From all those who cared

I'm starting to realize
Foolishly
I have just tried to hide

Away from my problems
Trying
To escape responsibility

And because of that
Silence
Broken only by the tide

I wanted to be an island
Thinking
My motives were pure

But now I know
Truly
I had selfish reasons

So I turn around
Hoping
For something to guide me home

I see a light in the distance
Surely
A sign of coming seasons

Author notes: I'm not sure why in society being the lone wolf or solitary figure is so sought for, maybe it's a macho thing or possibly it's just trying to be unique. I feel that for guys especially it's an accepted thought that admitting you need help is a sign of weakness. Be it pride or whatever this prevents so many people from actually asking for assistance when in reality it probably takes more guts to admit you're not enough alone.

Limitations

Why are limitations placed?
Upon those with dreams and ambitions
Those who only wish to explore their possibilities,
Instead of accepting the probabilities
Stats derived from calculations and studies
To scare those who wish to discover their potential

Constantly told that they will fail,
 There's no way to prevail,
And all the work ever done will be of no avail

When will we realize that stats mean nothing to the individual?
How will we know our future unless we take a chance?

So to the demoralized I say,
Break the cages, and shatter restrictions
The lies that were told, time to show your contradictions
To say you are here and capable of more
The passion you store is stronger than before
Now is the time to prepare for war

War on that which would hold you back,
The chains that bind, will never slack.
They'll continue to enclose until you're left in the black
They'll continue to constrict until you begin to attack

But the battle is not waged with weapons of subjugation
Rather it's fought with knowledge and determination
By those who grasp that they are a unique creation,
With such foundation, one day they'll find salvation

How do many still lack this revelation?

That we are all born for greatness,

What will it take for people to accept this?
When will we push forward and persist
Knowing that it's our purpose
To tell those who would resist
WE DO EXIST!

Author notes: I made a video to this poem with clips of Olympic athletes and regular people doing incredible things. Watching all the clips it's amazing to see the potential that the human body has when trained properly. Obviously not everyone can be track stars or weightlifters regardless of how they train, but there are so many aspects of "super human" abilities it's just a matter of finding one attainable to you and be determined to achieve it.

Productive

Commence the morning trumpet call
Awake the sleeping dreary all
Gather steadfast in the hall
To hear the ancient dictum
With every breath and through it all
Let time be not your victim

Leave emboldened from this place
Prepare for the upcoming race
Run with swiftness, strength and grace
Forever and again
Don't let pass or turn to waste
Firm course until the end

Be ardent with every stride
Passionate with humbled pride
Tenacious for those who've tried
Time is in your hands
Return to us as cultured guide
To show us foreign lands

Lead us to where you have been
Reveal to us the sights you've seen
And through it all may we glean
A sense of understanding
Time's start to end and all between
We must share in its commanding

Author Notes: This poem was created kind of in reverse as I heard a poem with
this rhyming device and I loved it. From there I mapped out how the poem would
rhyme without even knowing what the poem would be about. When the template
was done it was just a matter or filling in the blanks with the story.

Immaculate

Purpose

An average bird of average tones
With dappled greens and shades of stones
This bird has gone through life unseen

And with all the friends it's ever known
Their vibrant colours it's never shown
For it's just the colour of stone

Imagine the feeling of living in a rainbow
Knowing that you don't belong
Knowing that you don't add to the beauty
Believing that God got it wrong

This average bird of average size
Finds it difficult to merely rise
Above the flock it's always known

With strength and speed not so great
Makes it all the harder to break
Away from those who've been so close

Imagine the feeling, trying to find yourself
Unable to learn who you are
The peace needed to look within
As familiar as the distant star

This average bird with average goals
Now determined to break the moulds
Regardless of the price to pay

Desperate to find the purpose given
The reason why it keeps on living
It's now time to seize the day

Imagine the feeling, trying to break free
So you lift up your voice and sing
And soaring above the shouts and the screams
The song reaches the ears of the king

All around you the crowd is silent
As your voice continues to grow
The seas cease to be violent
For everyone that is around you know

This is a song written by angels
Given to us from the throne
And the one chosen to proclaim the message
Was an average bird the shade of stone

Author Notes: I am a firm believer that anyone can be used for greatness regardless of age gender or race. Sometimes it's just a matter of giving those who wouldn't normally have an opportunity a chance. It's why I enjoy shows like America's got talent, especially when they find extraordinary talent in unassuming people.

Responsibility

Why do some choose to be caught?
In a place where the battle has already been fought
In a land where the truth has already been sought
In a time where the lessons have already been taught
Why do they choose to stay in the same spot?
The only explanation is that they wish not
To leave behind a history of tyranny brought
But instead to place harmony in peoples' thought

For they remember why He came
And know in their hearts He would do the same
The lion who may not be tame
But will protect and love us all the same
Not for any amount of money or fame
Not because of pride or shame
But because of understanding that life isn't a game
And there's more to it then always passing the blame

So they take responsibility for their action
Despite the chance of their friends' retraction
Separating themselves from the major faction
By derailing safety from its moral traction
Hoping to create a sense of attraction
For a new system to find satisfaction
To give your entire effort, not just a fraction
In order to inspire a chain reaction

Salvation

Throughout my life I've try to find true joy
To battle the emptiness that slowly consumes my soul.
I try to find a solution to this ever growing problem
To be free from this burden, this un-payable toll.

Everything in this world has left me in want
I've never been satisfied with their temporary peace.
I pray for something more, for something everlasting
I pray this as I step upon death's withered heath.

Looking towards the ground from high atop my platform
I prepare for the unforgiving descent.
A moment before I take my final step
A glimmer of light appears in the distant.

Is this the answer I seek?
The solution to my problems finally revealed.
The light lifts the burden from my back
Now I learn that my fate is not sealed.

Thoughts of death are swept aside
As I make my way towards this light.
I care not that the journey is challenging
For my salvation is finally within my sight.

Author notes: I wrote this poem when I was younger and I remember when my mom read it at first she was a little concerned for me. She asked me if there was anything I was going through and I laughed because although the poem in the beginning is dark I have always been a happy person that enjoys life. I think it's important to write about issues even if you are not an expert on them so that you can express a positive message to people who relate to the darker side of what you write about.

Seasons

The sun is radiant and earth takes up a joyful song
Days are long and the light exposes every alcove
Children's laughter mingles with the sweet blossom scent
To trap these days forever are what most people dream

But soon despite the pleas the wind must begin to blow
Clouds begin to form in the sky that was clear
Trees take on the colour of fire and prepare for their sleep
Winds start to cool the air seems so different than before

Life seems to flee away from an unseen foe
Where once was vibrant is now still and quiet
Softly and without warning the descent begins
From the heavens crystal rain falls toward the earth

Encasing the world in a majestic mantle of white
Trees are bare the wind is harsh and stings the skin
All hope that we will be able to escape is lost
So cold the grasp, it tightens around the neck

Soon we cease to fight and accept the frozen bed
Our vision begins to blur and our eyes become heavy
We say one last prayer before we forever close our eyes
The waters freeze and all that is left is a deafening silence

But from the quiet all around us, a single sound is heard
A message of hope and renewal wrapped in this solitary note
At first all alone, but soon joined by many others
The promising sound of water droplets falling from the sky

Our frigid tomb begins to melt and our eyes become lighter
The song that was silenced begins to be heard through the air
As we become aware of warmth long forgot coming over the horizon
We stretch in anticipation for the arrival of the sun

Serenity

Stress is winning, breaking me down
If not helped soon, I'll be beyond saving
Upon the wind, I have heard talk
Of the emotion I have been craving

A sleeping power, to cure the restless
A miracle sought for since antiquity
A thought of peace, concept of calm
I seek the sensation known as serenity

So as a pilgrim, I dedicate my life
To begin my journey to find this notion
Focus minded, I will not be deterred
I will climb mountains, navigate the ocean

Full of optimism and eagerness
I search for this ideal able to heal my soul
Though forward my motion, reverse the effect
I seem to be drifting farther from my goal

I yearn for day, but delve deeper into night
Somehow my feet have left the course
One step forward, two steps back
No matter my action, I'm filled with remorse

My friends beg me to rest
But I persist, looking for path to take
I walk faster to keep ahead of the strain
But the harder I push, the more I ache

Still I push harder, now beginning to run
Peace less a privilege and more a need
My legs ache, I pay them no mind
I feel my want slowly turning to greed

Unable to run further I fall to the ground
But I begin to crawl, I will not fail
For as long as breath fills my lungs
I will continue to fight until I prevail

I soon reach the point of my limitation
My mind is willing, but my body too weak
So I lie on the dirt and accept my fate
For stress to come and the havoc it will wreak

I take a deep breath to prepare my soul
And wait... surprised by the silence I find
Another breath more soothing then the first
The calm before the storm caresses my mind

As I lay there, with eyes towards the sky
Patiently awaiting the doom of my soul
I can't help but feel a peace from on high
I wonder how I was able to find my goal

Stress never came, never found where I lay
For the first time in my life I felt free
Knowing what I had to do, I rose to my feet
To tell the story of how serenity found me

Author Notes: This poem was written after I lost my wallet with all of my identification in it and for weeks I couldn't find it. I tore through my room and house and revisited everywhere I could think of for those weeks and nothing came up. I like when you try to retrace your steps it's like a movie playing in your head and you're trying to relive what happens. Eventually I gave up looking for it and not 2 days after I was sitting on the couch and felt a little uncomfortable, checked behind the cushion and there it was, underneath me the whole time. I instantly related that experience to just the idea of searching for something and this poem came about.

Shadow

Withering days watching the creeping moss
It's impossible not to feel a sense of loss
Lost chances never to be regained
Lost time which the shadows have claimed

With sun sinking deep into the mountains
The shadows spill forth like water from fountains
Covering the ground with mighty force
Barriers unable to determine the course

Thick and silent the shadows slowly spread
With the flow of time, they are being fed
Soon growth from the black, hands reach out
Trying to take hold, to spread the doubt

Doubt in discovery, doubt in tomorrow
The shadow content to exist in sorrow
Resist becoming part of this destructive way
Do not become one lost to yesterday

Instead look ahead and grasp onto hope
Pull yourself forward with horizon's rope
Begin to explore what Destiny holds
Begin to write the story yet to be told

Remember the past but do not remain
Lest you give the shadow time to gain
Keep in mind through peace or assault
We are to be salt of the earth, not pillars of salt

Author Notes: Remembering the past is good and a very important thing to do, but I feel when you dwell on it to the extent that it prevents you from moving forward is when it can be hazardous.

Shining Bright

The sun warms our faces
It brightens all places
Where there is sorrow
It eliminates the traces

It soothes every sore
Penetrates the very core
With every new rotation
Who knows what's in store

Will it be roaring?
Radiant orb soaring?
As long as the sun is out
I know it won't be boring

But during times of grey sky
Clouds obstruct beams on high
That the sun has disappeared
Often we fall for this lie

We may believe the sun is gone
But its' light still shines on
Beyond thick floating curtain
As radiant and ever strong

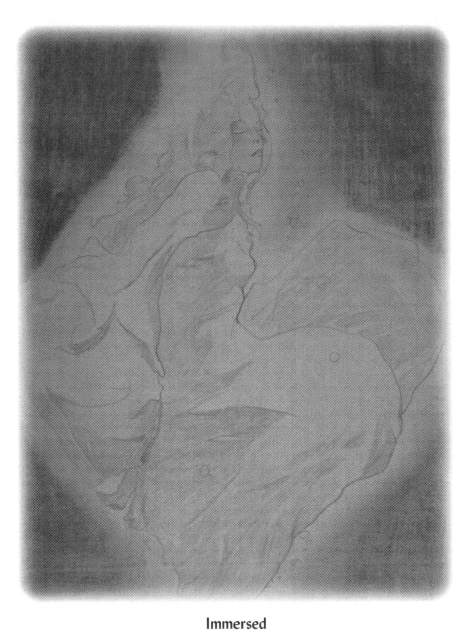

Immersed

The Crystal Rose

I have gone astray
Apart from all I know
Stuck in a pit of solitude and dismay

Now my only choice
To return to the light
Is to scale the cliffs so again I may rejoice

I climb for many days
From the valley of the lost
I begin to feel that I have found my way

But as I reach the height
Of this mountain in my life
I am still lost, seeing no familiar place in sight

But in my darkest hour
You show yourself to me
Illuminating my heart, a seemingly simple flower

My precious crystal rose
Your existence an enigma
Your splendour the likes of which a few will ever know

Your petals gleam fire
A beauty unrivalled
So pure a radiance, its strength will never tire

I apologize to stare
But I am compelled to stay
For in this world a beauty such as yours is rare

On the mountainside
Eternally hidden from the world
I hope you will be kind enough to allow me to also hide

Hide away from my fears
From the pain and stresses of life
Spared the moments filled with the many sorrowful tears

But why do you exist?
This question consumes my mind
One that I can assure will not be quickly dismissed

Are you for the weak?
The lonely or broken hearted
Of for those in which beauty is all they seek

Dwelling on these questions
For length of time unknown
I have noticed many things about you worth mention

Despite the sting of rain
Or the darkest nights
Your splendour and purity has never experienced stain

To take you for my own
I would never again be lost
And never again would I feel like I was alone

And to its fear
At my heart's desire
The moon begins to weeps silver tears

As the tears of sorrow
Fall gently on my face
I realize why you must stay here for the rest of tomorrows

You exist for many reasons

To give hope and strength
To the travelers who cross your path season after season

So now from you I will part
And return home renewed
I will never forget you for I take you in my heart

Making sure everyone knows
What you have done for me
And where to find you, my precious crystal rose

The Path Before Me

I choose to walk down rough trodden path
A decision made for me rather than at my request
In my hand a seed, a purpose unknown
I place it in my pocket and worry not its cost

Rows of colossal trees guard my travels
To the left and right wooden titans watching over me
Each grown from a seed now mighty and healthy
Guiding my steps that I may not become lost

Those who have walked before me, I may never know
But they have left their mark upon the stone
I follow the footsteps of the previous generations
But I leave my own memories to guide those that follow

With every stride, I begin to move faster
I notice my footprints getting larger with each step
I come across a tree that once was strong and vibrant
But now cracked and fallen for inside was only hollow

Stopping in my tracks, the image startling
I ponder its meaning, soon realizing to take my time
Knowing that if I rush without chance of growth
I will become just as hollow as that once mighty tree

Soon the path before me begins to widen
Covering the ground like the light of the horizon
The trees that enclosed the path have abruptly stopped
Suddenly my trail is not as clear as it used to be

Too many footsteps to follow and explore each set
I feel torn as to which path I should go
I look everywhere for help, but all I see
Scattered on the ground many seeds like my own

Some discarded carelessly by their owner
Others planted quickly without care
All left unguarded to be eaten by the birds
Never will those seeds grow for they were never sown

Eager to explore the land of possibilities
In my heart I am tempted to do the same
But I look to the seeds that could have become trees
And the guidance they could have given to those yet to be

Determined not to dismiss my charge
My seed is planted with love and care
And with the past taken care in a firm foundation
I make for expanse to walk my own path before me

The Race

As you draw near
Make your mind clear
For the race in which you compete is about to begin
Slow your breath
Prepare to outrun death
You will have to give everything in order to win

The crowd cheers your name
Though some angry that you came
Those who wish to break your spirit making you easy to attack
But pay them no heed
Focus on what you need
A willing mind and fervent soul when you step upon the track

Your mark is set
May you never forget
All the training you have endured to make it this far
Show them your might
Your eagerness to fight
And how capable you are at raising the bar

Your muscles tense
As you begin to sense
The starting pistol bring raised into distant sky
With instant explosion
Fearsome propulsion
To the gun being fired this is your body's reply

You run so fast
No wind blows past
For you cut through the air like a diamond knife
But you hear the sound
Of opponents gaining ground
Eager to take away the ambitions of your life

You stumble and fall
You know you've lost it all
It's just a matter of time before the other racers overtake
But pursuing feet halt
You look to see the fault
At the sight of outstretched hands you realize your mistake

You notice your crest
Is upon each runners chest
The entire time you have been trying to outrun your own team
You take the nearest hand
It helps you to stand
As you hear each one urging you to chase after your dream

They offer you the lead
But you know there's no need
For your senses are now realigned with what's truly essential
With your team you run
To catch the setting sun
As now you realize you can explore your full potential

Writers Block

How do you deal when your mind is spent?
Always giving with no time given to resent
Ideas float above but just out of grasp
Mind desperately sore caught in empty clasp

An ailment common to those who write
Discovering inspiration, a constant fight
Works laced with words to many unknown
Hoping to give meaning to an effort scarcely grown

Randomly piecing together a tapestry of incoherent thought
Just to make a deadline to be published and bought
Sending out art forms, without heart's permission
Becoming slaves to pressure, knowing only submission

Where can you find stimulation when the well is dry?
When muses are beyond reach, despite how you try
There has to be a place where ideas choose to dwell
A space of infinite, undreamt stories to tell

I tell you the secret; I have found this place
A land of inspiration, of freedom and grace
Almost missed it for it exists where we begin
Not the realm of sensory perception, but within

Hiding in the quiet shadows of our soul
Frightened by the worldly noise as a whole
Longing for stillness unnatural to those of today
In the quiet it chooses to stay

So find Stone Island amidst peaceful river
Imagine the use of parchment and quiver
Lay in grassy bed beneath towering tree
Rest to the breeze; allow your mind to be free

Colours of light will separate before your eyes
Hidden possibilities eager to be realized
Let imagination take control, forget formalities
Set upon the task to break all realities

Author Notes: This poem is ironic because I wrote it after just finishing quite a lot of material for various things I was working on and I ran into writer's block myself. Any student or writer can relate to this and if you don't know what it is, if you have ever caught yourself staring at a blank piece of paper and in your head the only thing you can think about is "I'm staring at a blank piece of paper" then you have writer's block. I went to my friend and told her I need some inspiration and she told me why don't you write about not being able to write? Almost instantly I began writing this poem and it came pretty much all in one sitting. When I finished it I thought "might as well take advantage of this momentum", but when I tried to start a new poem I got hit with the block again haha.

Chapter 2: Observation

Blindness

Waking with no sight to calm your heart
Waking to a morning as dark as night
Sounds become pieces of a puzzle yet created
Trying to build a world in your mind that makes sense
Interesting how most people face that challenge
Trying to grasp the realities that life has to offer
Blind not in sight but of the truth
Searching for answers only believing with proof

In a way you are more free then those who see
For the world in your mind is as you see fit
Not restrained by the structure of biases and judgements
The effect of one's appearance non-existent
To those who were born with sight never given
I wonder when they realize that they are different
That not all have been dealt the cards they hold
Would they realize if they were never told?

I can close my eyes to envision my heart's desires
I can imagine places that I have never seen
Can you do the same; can you see with your mind?
Can you do as we do and imagine in kind?
For some only live in worlds of black and white
But what about those who live in shadow less sight?
In the greys of creativity where rules don't exist
Where our understanding struggles to subsist

I ask all this not to glorify or make light
Of your circumstances or your daily fight
But to give sight to those with narrow understanding
Who have lived content to judge others by branding
To destroy stereotypes so barriers can be broken
To pave a way for the truth to be spoken
Let this message for tomorrow ring true
To look upon this world with each other's point of view

Authors Notes: Now it's probably just me but sometimes I will walk around with my eyes closed just to see how well I can navigate areas. It usually ends with me almost running into someone or tripping over a random object but it always impresses me how blind people can get about. I heard of this one blind kid who has developed a form of echo location to help him see quite effectively and that pretty much blew me away. If that story is true and they could teach it to blind people then the world would be a better place. (slightly louder with all the clicking) but better nonetheless.

Democracy

Lust for power
Disdain for democracy
How can we stand for this outright mockery?

Mockery of the system
Mockery of the vote
We have been told we got it wrong
And now we are no longer of note

The people spoke and for a moment were heard
But little did we know, in the background what stirred

Three, once the number of much that is good
Now responsible for something that never should

The change of government without the people's voice
The change of our leadership without giving us a choice

What should we do?
Should we take a seat?
Wait for them to meet?
Those who claim themselves elite
Those who claim they should not have been beat

As for me
Well I refuse to wait
For someone else to dictate
What things I should contemplate
While they are trying to become weavers of fate

Instead I choose to stand, hand in hand
With all those willing to band
For a system of the people we will demand
With a voice, a choice heard throughout the land

Gone is the time that we will be lead by hypocrisy
Give us what we deserve, our right to democracy

Just a Question

I have a hypothetical question
That I feel the need to mention
A thought that deserves attention
To expand its comprehension

Is it right to teach the daughter and son
To accept the races of everyone
In order to see stereo types undone
And stop those who feel the need to shun

When because of our selfish pride
We have learned to abide
To rules purposed to easily divide
Those who don't follow our stride

When asked about it, we tend to lie
Saying that truly we use to try
To see things eye to eye
But eventually gave up and said goodbye

Because we found it so hard to do
When we tried to share our point of view
Only to have them in our minds misconstrue
The evidence and facts we believed to be true

These double standards are not fair
The only way to teach children to care
Is to lead by example and be aware
That we are sought for guidance everywhere

Author notes: One of the biggest things I can't stand is hypocrisy and even more so when the committers try to make lame excuses for their actions. Now it's one thing to try and look out for someone you care about but I think most of the time the reasons are that people are too concerned of their public image. If you truly care about someone and want them to stop what they are doing although you are in the same boat I feel it would be more beneficial if you admitted it and try to help each other through the ordeal.

Little Boxes

Little boxes stacked upon the ledge
Each little box sitting on the edge
To these little boxes we do pledge
Our money, our focus, our time

Carrying what we can't live without
Their promises never do we doubt
To our weekly shopping we are devout
Eager to give every dime

Depicting many experiencing joys
From famous magazines to childish toys
Capturing the hearts of girls and boys
Should it be considered a crime?

Or should we choose instead to teach
That happiness is never out of reach
And practice what we decide to preach
That life itself is sublime

Perspective

They say no news is good news because most news is bad
Articles ineffective unless readers get mad
How many make a living showing how the world is so wrong
How many start their day listening to their distressing song
Now I'm not disillusioned, ignorant or naïve
I just choose to view things differently then they perceive
The world is not perfect, far from it to speak true
But what is griping and complaining going to do?
Some see me as an inexperienced, wishful thinker
I'd rather be that then hardened, fuming and bitter
Let's acknowledge our weaknesses but focus on our strengths
We live only because of those who went through great lengths
Let's seek out and recognize people that strive to do good
Celebrate large and small victories in the ways we should
Let's bring notice and fame to stories of citizens getting it right
Reports that make our mornings go from dreary to bright
Who knows, maybe a positive attitude can begin to spread
And where we would criticize we will try to improve instead

Author Notes: Whenever I read the newspaper on my way to work the majority of the stories are depressing and tragic. Yes it's important to know what is going on in the world and not be ignorant but at the same time I feel "what's the point?" I mean we all read the same stories about atrocities at home and abroad, get mad and then flip to the next story, forgetting about what we just read. If you want to be concerned pick one thing to be concerned about and then try to help solve that problem rather than grumbling about everything and doing nothing. There should be a happy newspaper that publishes encouraging and uplifting stories throughout with one "tragic" story of the day with things you can do to help in the article; I wonder how effective that would be?

Terminology

English is truly fascinating
A mixture of metaphors and sayings
From countries far away
A collaboration of cultures
I know little about
With words for every occasion
To express joy, resent, excitement or doubt
The possibilities seemingly endless
Our thoughts clearly portrayed
Articulated in ways
To let those who hear what we say
Know our point of view
And whether they choose to disagree
Or they believe them to be true
Soon their thoughts will be expressed anew

A child learning to laugh, adorable
A country at war with itself, tragic
A bear escapes from the zoo, unnerving
An evening with the one you love, magic

With so many words at our disposal
I feel many are forgotten or merely undiscovered
Deep and rich parts of speech
To accurately depict are truest desires

For example let me paint a scene
A simple bench by lake serene
With lovely company, night pristine
Clouds above, but rain unseen

A mighty flash illuminates the sky
Violet lightning splintered up high
Shooting through the clouds nearby
Phenomenal… my only reply

So I implore you to explore
New terms to express a great deal more
Instead of reject, use abjure
Unequivocal to say you're sure
Cataract instead of waterfall
Prevaricate to substitute "trying to stall"

Let's seek out new terminology
To demonstrate our true ideology

Author notes: Playing scrabble or boggles with my brother Steve or my Aunt Ruth is frustrating because their vocabulary is ridiculous. Whenever I play with them I have to have a dictionary with me to check if they are cheating but they never are! There should be some rule about being happy scoring 12 points on a word and then the next player comes right after with some 50 pointer looking all smug. If for nothing else I urge you to expand your vocabulary so when playing these "family fun" games, you will be on even footing.

My quiet place

In my quiet place I will spend
Hours upon days on end
In this quiet place I shall sleep
And pray to God my soul shall keep

And in this quiet place I can hear
Angels singing profoundly clear
A thousand whispers upon the breeze
Singing with undiscovered keys

In my quiet place I can feel
Softened earth beneath hardened heel
Unsure path walked by many before
My future uncertain, unopened door

In this quiet place I can see
Glimpses of my destiny
Visions caught atop the lake
Revealed like waves that slowly break

In my quiet place I can stay
To face the world, I can delay
But I must leave to earn my worth
A mirror to reflect light upon the earth

Author Notes: I usually carry around with me a little notepad to jot down ideas and lines I think of throughout the day. Before I did this I would come up with so many rhymes to use and forget them by the time I got home. Like a comedian I heard say, then you spend the next hour trying to convince yourself that what you thought of and forgot wasn't clever in the first place. Luckily while I was working at a camp sitting by the lake I did have my pad on me because looking out with the breeze and the sun on my face, this poem pretty much wrote itself.

Inside and out

Revelation

I happened across this powerful revelation
Concerning the matter of our current situation
I fear that if we continue down our present direction
We will all be greatly surprised at the destination

Now it's not surprising if you choose to evaluate any nation
When people choose to follow the ways of greed and deception
Many think they know the truth but it's all a misconception
Letting others tell them what's real and mould their perception

Some are so concerned with making the right impressions
That they sacrifice what's right in order to feed their obsessions
Instead of looking at the big picture, they live life session by session
Content at being happy now despite their future of oppression

The world is full of those who give outward appearances too much
        attention
Focusing on looks when the real problem isn't even on the physical
        dimension
When we gather to discuss, the important matters people forget to
        mention
And we wonder why things don't get better and there's this ever
        growing tension

Hopefully these few lyrics offer some sort of motivation
To go out and attack the real problems without thought of hesitation
In order to make a bright future of our very own creation
Steering away from destruction I saw in my powerful revelation

A Simple Smile

A smile released into the sky
Changed are those who see
Signal of joy to passerby
Prisoners weighed down set free
Why genuine grin, has power when shown
The reasons studied but still unknown

What secrets lie within a smile?
What purpose does it represent?
A show of peace, to reconcile
Or to display concealed resent
A two edged sword unconfined
Each user to choose how it's defined

I've seen a smile in everyway
One expression to express so much
Able to melt cold hearts away
Or have kingdoms torn with such
To convey inner thought without a word
To express intent and remain unheard

What reasons will you smile today?
To encourage or deceive
Be reminded when you portray
What you give you shall receive
A two edged sword unconfined
Each user to choose how it's defined

Author notes: It's weird how people react to a smile, especially strangers that you just pass by on the street. I try smiling to random people just to see what they do and the majority of the time they smile back even though they have no idea who I am and why I am smiling at them. Although I would like to mention, the reaction you get is also determined by the type of smile you give out (some people have some awfully creepy smiles). Going with this I asked some of my friends what a smile means to them and with their feedback I realised how versatile smiles can be. I want to thank Anika, Dianne, and Bernadette for helping me with this one.

To the Youth

Try to contemplate the words entering your mind
Ideals of a kingdom eager to bind

Allowing the words of false idols to fill your thought
Erasing moral fabric that each should be taught

Venom mixed with honey to sound sweet to the ear
A clever poison taken by many without fear

No fear for there's no knowledge of what's taking place
But bitterness and resent's the only lasting taste

Where's the uplifting song with encouraging rhyme?
Where are the moral activists after making prime time?

Responsibility is given whether you like it or not
So spread truth and hope before we're all caught

In the baseless lie that life isn't worth living
Let's turn things around, let's begin by giving

Author Notes: Music is powerful and anyone who disagrees probably has
no emotions at all. When different styles of music can affect your mood, it's
something to think about. I myself am pretty eclectic and my playlists are usually
a mixture of genres put together which is why it doesn't surprise me when I go
from relaxed to amped when I hear a rock song follow a mellow reggae tune.
My brother Matt jokes that if the army could play his favourite rock song inside
an army helmet somehow, he would go off and fight anything. With music being
so powerful we should be careful what we expose our ears too.

Two Kingdoms

There was a place where two kingdoms reigned
From the land, both were well sustained
To the north, they lived by a lake pristine
To the south, amongst forests of emerald green

The plains of vision separated the two
An expanse that would take hours to pass through
But though the journey simple from forest to lake
None from either tribe ever bothered to take

No one could see the point in visiting the other
They clung to their homes like children to their mother
"We have all of our needs and wants fulfilled"
"Why leave it all, just so relations we can build?"

So for many years the people from lake and wood
Kept to themselves and believed life to be good
But then a catastrophe swept across the land
Trees withered and died, the waters turned to sand

Immediately those who once lived by the trees
Sent out messengers to the lake with desperate pleas
But at the same time those who knew of water
Sent letters to the woods with their sons and daughters

And during this time when unity was expected
Instead the leaders of each kingdom simply rejected
Refusing for fear of losing the little they had left
For fear that soon their lives would be bereft

And just as it seemed that life would cease to be
Descending from heaven a light for all to see
Settling upon a great mountain in the distance
For the kingdoms a sign of hope and renewed existence

Scouts were sent out in order to discover
The secrets of the light, the truths it would uncover
And the sight awaiting the explorers from afar
Water cascading stone, beneath a fragment star

With speed of mighty eagles, the riders returned home
To explain to their kings the blessing they were shown
A great waterfall with plants and food galore
An oasis in the dessert with no need to want for more

Without hesitation abandoned became the begotten wood
As those by the empty lake followed as fast as they could
Setting out to together to claim this land of prosperity
So they might see their futures in brighter clarity

Along the way an unexpected miracle occurred
A notion that not long ago was thought to be absurd
For the two tribes began walking side by side
And without notice their lives started to coincide

Sharing stories of their homes they grew closer together
As spirits remained high as did the weather
Accompanied by clear sky and shining sun above
Soon all could see paradise, the gift given with love

New homes were built and the two tribes were as one
Many saw this as a sign of life just begun
But despite the peace and harmony that existed
The minds of the two kings became quite twisted

Sceptical that this new land would be able support all
They devised ways to ensure the other kingdom would fall
In cold of night, each king gathered his people near
And declared in the morn they would battle steel with spear

Although the citizens unwilling to fight for the reason
They all prepared for war as to not commit treason
With broken hearts and silent mouths each raised their sword
Facing turmoil inside consciences suppressed and ignored

With battle trumpets sounding the armies charged and cried
Knowing that with the setting sun many they loved will have died
And with thunderous force, the two kingdoms collided
A war solely fought by the greedy, scared and misguided

Saddened by the conflict grey turned the star that was revered
Ascending back into heaven as waterfall disappeared
All dropped their weapons and stared at now bare rock wall
Finding a simple message reading "Salvation for all"

Author Notes: This is one of my favourite poems that I wrote because I love telling stories to convey my thoughts. The poet Homer has to be one of my favourite writers for his works like the Iliad, an epic poem as long as a novel depicting a huge ancient Greek adventure. After reading the Iliad and hearing an old song on the radio called "one tin soldier" by coven that has such a powerful story behind it, I was inspired to write this poem. Hopefully I can eventually write an epic poem like the Iliad in the future, I guess I will have to wait and see if my mind can rhyme for that long and keep readers entertained.

Chapter 3: Love

Dialogue

We have lived in this garden for so long
But my love for you has never been so strong
Your beauty brings tears of joy to my eye
That to keep you safe I would choose to die

Flattering words as these you have spoken before
Are empty promises all you have, or is there more?
All I ask is to be free from this wretched place
A paradise to others but only a prison in our case

You know it is impossible for us to leave
The hopelessness of it causes me to grieve
So I dwell on the simple pleasures that I possess
Eyes to see, lips to speak, and ears to hear your breath

I try to view things as you have managed to do
But in the end, my heart cannot deny what is true
No matter how beautiful this garden may be
It doesn't change that we are trapped for eternity

I would rather be confined with a purpose of my own
Than to live a life of freedom with one never known
We were created into an image of perfection
And set here to protect this place of reflection

We were set here without question of our desire
Set her for the sole purpose that we would never tire

Is it your wish that you were never made?

I wish that I was given a chance to play

...From the beginning our situation has never been fair
But the thought of losing you is too much for me to bear

You have been loyal to me; your love has never waned
To part from you, would cause my heart to be strained

So what is it that your are trying to say

That if I must live here for the rest of my days
My love, I would pick no other to share the view

Thanks, I love you too

-Dialogues of the garden statues

Author Notes: While I was working on this piece in my mind I wondered what exactly is speaking. At first I thought of forbidden lovers like Romeo and Juliet then I thought well it's a poem so I can give voice to anything I want. I played with the idea of the conversation being between flowers, then animals and finally I saw the garden statue in my mom's garden and was sold. I love twists and hopefully when you read the poem, the end of it through you for a loop. Read the poem again now knowing what is speaking and see if it makes sense.

Heart's Pledge

To the one so tender and true

I pledge my heart to only you

To be your shelter from the storm

To be your light in darkest night

To be the lifter of your dreams

To be your shining armoured knight

This pledge I say to only you

Your eyes alone

Your heart alone

That when all is said and through

Remember my heart will be with you

Author Notes: This is probably one of the first "short" poems I wrote. For some reason I used to think that poems had to be at least a page long to be considered decent and to get my point across, but then when I started reading poetry from famous writers, I got to see a lot of poems no longer then a few stanzas. Although they were short they had punch and I liked the effect so I decided to write similarly. That and when I tried to get my friends to read my longer stuff they were like, woah! that's a lot of words for me to read right now, so then I figured I would tackle some short ones for them.

Inside and out

As pearls on a necklace
Or blossoms on a tree
These beautiful things
Are like you to me

Precious objects
Handled with greatest care
Fragrant aroma
Drifting through the air

The burning stars
Suspended in night skies
Attempt to compare
With the brilliance of your eyes

Your youthful vitality
And young looking ways
Will remain with you
For the rest of your days

But more impressive still
Is what you have inside
Your character and compassion
Towards all those alive

A bountiful love
You share with all you meet
Be it family or friends
Or someone just met on the street

For beauty also lies
Within the heart
And you've shown this
From the very start

So never be doubtful
Hear me as I shout
You are beautiful
Inside and Out

Author Notes: Beauty is a complex thing that really has no answer. I mean
the beholder is truly the person who determines what is beautiful or not and
everyone likes different things for different reasons. It's funny when you see
movies that show "unattractive" people as being beautiful on the inside and
"hot" people as really being jerks. This is sometimes true but there are also
times when a person is "unattractive" on the outside and the inside or a "hot"
person that is genuinely nice. You can't judge someone by their looks and that
goes both ways.

Inspiration

Why and how did poetry start?

What compelled the first poet's heart?

An ideal? A thought? An exotic muse?

What was the flame to ignite the fuse?

As for me it is clearly the last

An angel whose light she chose to cast

To pierce the cloud that hides my way

To show the path from day to day

In the storm she is steady hand

For her I long to be a better man

Mesmerized

I saw you from the corner of my eye
Through the crowd, there you stood
So captivating your every move
Gliding above floor made of wood

As music dances through the air
So your feet match each step
Constantly in and out of view
Like truth revealed or secret kept

Only fleeting glimpses of your face
I piece together your intent
Cautiously moving ever closer
Soon I know your fragrant scent

It takes my mind to welcome place
A summer's day with playful wind
I close my eyes, stand still and breath
Slowing down time to take it in

As I return to where we are
Still I dream to my surprise
There you stand beauty unrivalled
My heart forever mesmerized

Meticulous

Trust in me, entirely
When your heart is lost
For I will search humanity
Regardless of the cost
Charged with such a vital case
To find the smile that left your face
I will search for joy and bring it to this place
You will laugh again

I will journey and explore
The sea of endless sand
Make my way unto the core
Sift with steady hand
I will never fall to fear
Be around to catch each tear
For I know when the dust is clear
You'll soon sing my friend

To the ocean, I'll pursue
Each wave and crest and swell
Wonders proven true
But I won't stay to dwell
For I simply can't afford
Being kept from going toward
Finding your smile is my reward
Your heart will surely mend

But my limits are not bound
To the earthly plane
I will stay, till I have found
Your smile in heaven's domain
Through my search I will not miss
Despite of how ridiculous
For you I'll be meticulous
To find your smile again

Author Notes: This poem is part of what I call my one word poems, as I often ask a good friend of mine for interesting words to make a poem out of. Usually when I get a word from her something pops in my head automatically and this was no exception. Sometimes I feel writers only want to express a single idea, sentence or word, but know that alone it might be looked past so they create a large piece of work to bring attention to that single thought they wish to express.

Moonchild

Beneath the willow tree, atop the hill
The beach before me, calm and still
Each night I come to view the one able to capture my heart
The moon stands still in anticipation
To view the heavenly inspiration
And hear her song of angelic praise and the joy that it imparts

Water begins to foam and break
As she emerges from crystal lake
The moon glows brighter in her presence, I long to be at her side
Endowed with mantle of pure white
A glorious embodiment of silver light
Walking through the sands of time amongst the gentle tide

Though the distance between us great
Looking at her, I know every trait
A patient loving heart with a gentle caring mind
She moves toward me closer still
My body moves against my will
I follow my heart so I will learn if she sees me in kind

Drawing near, I see her face
Her smile, warm as mother's embrace
She says hello, never has that word meant so much
The sand beneath me disappears
The soothing tide I no longer hear
The only thing on my mind is to feel this angel's touch

As quickly as she appeared in grace
She vanishes without a trace
Taking with her my heart to leave me alone in reality
I just walk away and grin
As I whisper into the wind
When you need to find me, I'll be beneath the willow tree

Masterpiece

My Life's Goal

Mother, the name whispered within the womb
To ease my heart that I may drift to sleep
Mother, the thought I have always known
Before I could talk or consciousness grown

The one before the start
So near to my heart
The beat of every breath
Soothing to caress

This love you showed me before you could hold me
Hold me gently in your arms
The sacrifices made to ensure the pathway paved
Paved free from earthly harms

The one I had to leave to know
            had to see to grow
                        had to touch to show
All the love I have for you

Now although I can't remember my first years on earth
I'm sure I can guess my feelings from birth
That curious stare, all I could do then to show I care
That look of love I gave to you alone
That look forever yours to own

But now that I am old enough to express inner thought
I've entered into the realm of expression and sought
Ways to convey my joy, gratefulness and thanks

But there are no words to articulate my feelings
So instead I will push to become a better child
I will strive so my love for you will never be outdone
I will push towards this goal above all others
So that you will know how important it is for me to say
You are my mother

Author Notes: On mother's day I wrote this and gave it to my mom taking extra care to use tea bags and a candle to make the page look antique with a brown hue and burnt edges. I learned how to make paper look old in grade school and I find I use that skill more often than a large amount of what I learned back then, go figure. I wonder why we like making things look antique as if that would add to the value or importance; I blame the Antiques Road show for this way of thinking.

Rings Of Love

Precious metals from the earth
Showered with flames to make pure
Given new purpose through rebirth
To the shattered heart, a blessed cure

Forged to be a symbol of love
This dear sentimental token
Beloved item heralds write of
The showing of one's heart outspoken

Your love as these rings you hold
Representing the care you've known
Firm, never ending, tender and bold
Beautiful, elegant, tasteful and shown

Your love as these rings you wear
Belong to the one who placed it
Handled with gentleness and care
Your souls combined, a perfect fit

Forever be her knight in shining armour
Be the inspiration to his every dream
Quick to protect her virtue and honour
His place of peace beside the stream

Now is the time to raise voices and sing
Eager to see what the future will bring
Through cold winters and warm springs
Let your love remain as these very rings

So Close, So Far

You look upon her from afar
You the moon, she the star
Heavenly bodies with destinies intertwined
To star gazers it would appear
Star and moon so very near
But the truth we know is rarely so kind

Stepping closer to hear her sound
You the clouds, she the ground
Coexisting for all times yet living parallel lives
Clouds turn grey with grief
Moments of contact far too brief
Reaching with lightning to find where she resides

Closer still the one who sought her
You the leaf and she the water
Aspects of the cycle longing to fill empty space
Even if leaf was to break free
To fall on lake beneath the tree
Only shallow relationships would be the case

Now face to face with beauty pure
You are him and she is her
People like nature living in separate space and time
But unique to humans alone
Are the souls that we each own
With power to break the rules to know love sublime

Author Notes: I wanted to create a feeling when writing this poem of getting ever closer but still remaining hopelessly apart. Sometimes goals in life often give the same feeling. It's as if we are making progress towards achieving our goal but ultimately we haven't really made much headway either because new obstacles arise or things we previously needed changes. Only the determined who choose to persevere despite changing circumstances end up getting what they want.

Souls Entwined

Two candles as one, two candles as one
A new life just begun, two candles as one
A promise to the sun, that when all is said and done
Your love will be these two candles as one

It's radiance to guide you through uncertain future
To reveal paths that lay before your feet
Your devotion to each other will feed the flame
Becoming inspiration to all those you meet

At first a faint glow, fragile and fair
Nurture it to grow, with patience and care
And I know through times of tears and pain
Your adoration to one another will never wane

May this candle burn bright
To be a beacon in the night,
Providing you both with clarity and sight

Two candles as one
Strong as silken thread spun
Two candles as one
The warmth never undone

Be prepared for that strength will be tested
The world will creep with mighty gale
To extinguish the flame you've dearly protected
But through it all I know you'll prevail
And show the world candle glow reflected
Shining eternal without sign of fail

Chapter 4: Diverse

Alphabetical Morning

Almost every day when I awake
Before I stretch, yawn and shake
Casually a mental check I'll take
Deciding on what choices to make

Eventually I will get out of bed
Flex my muscles, scratch my head
Guessing what the weatherman said
Hoping I have something clean in red

I go to the bathroom to wash my face
Judge myself in mirror, I take first place
Keeping in mind to set the pace
Letting myself know I'll win the race

Moving to kitchen so I can eat
Nothing appetizing until eyes meet
Oreo's. Family pack, how deliciously sweet
Probably good idea if I take a seat

Quickly I grab the morning news
Reading top headlines that amuse
Selecting a few articles to peruse
Try to skip the stories that confuse

Up from table, I head to the door
Very smoothly walk across the floor
Wonder what the day has in store
X rays for work grabbed from the drawer

Yell to the world I'm on my way
Zealously ready to begin my day

Author Notes: This one was fun to write just by mere concept. I'm not sure where I got the idea to write a 26 line poem that's alphabetical but I'm glad I did. As you can imagine some letters were harder to fit in fluidly than others but thank goodness for the invention of X-rays. X really hurt my head trying to find something that worked with the rest of the poem, it's no wonder it scores so much in scrabble.

Friend of Mine

Always gentle, always kind
When I think of a friend, you come to mind
No matter the situation, you're always there
Showing others the meaning of how to care

Always compassionate, always ready
You're the hand that keeps the weak steady
Unselfishness be your middle name
For you, morality and life be one and the same

Always prepared, always sacrificing
Your presence is considered by all a blessing
Supportive to all those in need
Honesty and trustworthiness your creed

Always gentle, always sincere
Willing to help others overcome their fears
Encouraging friends when no one else will believe
You constantly give without expectations to receive

Always joyful, always strong
Many can attest to your unwavering bond
To those with injured hearts, you help to mend
I am grateful for being able to call you my friend

I am the moon

I am the moon
Mysterious
In all that I do

The midnight beacon
Seeker
Of what is true

Sharing the sky
Though
Never out shun

A fleeting image
Enjoy
Before I'm gone

Constant in motion
Changing
As seasons turn

Ever watchful
Eager
To adapt and learn

I observe situations
Viewing
The ebb and flow

Offering guidance
Humbly
With the little I know

By shedding light
Bringing
Attention to the sky

Revealing that dreams
Truly
Are never too high

Author Notes: The inspiration for this poem came from my cousin Phillip when I showed him my poem "The Island" which is also found in this book. After reading it he said he liked it but also added that everyone uses islands as metaphors. He told me, "you have to go against the curve pick something obscure". After all that I decide to write about the moon... I'm not as obscure as I would like to be sometimes.

Knighthood

Fed stories of heroism
Won on battlefield
A young squire believes
For knighthood he was made

Practicing day and night
Without sign of yield
He strives to become great
Master of the blade

Soon his teacher calls
To help prepare for war
The squire arms his master
And waits in distance to learn

Watching armoured knights
Fight in chaotic core
Triumphant warriors emerge
Their faces sorrowed and stern

Running towards his mentor
The squire eagerly asks
"You do not shout in triumph?
You do not celebrate the fight?"

The knight stares at the boy
Mind gripped by recent task
Saying "poor lad you are blind
Naive, but I will give sight"

"Your impression of war false
The stories you heard, made up
What I have seen with these eyes
I pray this life for none of mine"

"But I take sword in hand
And with death I sup
Marching forward into battle
So they'll not have to do in kind"

"Please heed these words
And learn to wisely wield
Do not forge a path that robs
But instead choose to give"

With new understanding
The squire grasps sword and shield
To battle against the enemy
So that the innocent may live

Author Notes: This is one of my poems that I have in mind to do a trilogy of. As mentioned earlier I love to write poetry that tells a story to get my thoughts across. Rolling with the idea that poems can be like books I thought what is stopping me of writing sequels or prequels to things that I write about? Hopefully I can complete these continuations shortly in the future.

Last Class

So begins the hardest battle of my day
The final obstacle that blocks my way
The bane of my existence; how long will it last?
Prolonger of captivity, the day's final class

To prepare my mind, I check hanging clock
Placed above the door, I feel each tempting toc
Each tic as if to say, "time is slowing down"
The minute hand moving the wrong way around

I force myself to focus; the time reads 1:53
Just a little over an hour and then I'll be free
To keep myself busy, I open tattered book
Thinking I may as well give the work a look

But shortly I find the words put before me
Cause my eyes to grow tired and dreary
Before all this reading costs me my sight
I stare out the window to view natural light

Taken to a land where I am able to fly
I dream of soaring through the clouds nearby
A cough from my friend breaks my trance
I nod thanks and give the teacher a glance

As the lesson continues I truly try my best
Knowing all this work will be on the final test
I strain my ears to make out the teacher's sounds
All I hear is the womp womp from Charlie Brown

With the teacher speaking a language unknown
I decide to write notes to "get in the zone"
But I find the edges of my paper awkwardly bare
Doodling along the border to give it some flair

These tedious tasks are driving me insane
Surely class has a little time to remain
As I check the time, my hope takes a dive
Above the door the clock reads 1:55

Author Notes: This poem takes the adage a watched pot never boils and throws it into a situation pretty much everyone can relate to. How often have I been at work, school or someplace for a long period and felt the majority of time rush by until it's just about time to leave. I don't know if it's by some cruel joke or some magical force we can't explain but I argue that time literally slows down. One of these days I want to time the last few minutes of the work day just to see how long they actually last, I shall inform you all with my findings.

The Fisherman

Look upon the master fisherman as he prepares to leave the shore
His gaze turns to the mighty waves, but he pays no heed to their roar

Pushing off into his sturdy craft with only a fishing rod at his side
He begins the hunt for the legendary catch not for money, fame or
      pride

In the ocean he feels at home, the uneasy waters symbolize his life
In change and challenge he sees opportunity where others see strife

The scent of the creature fills his mind as he scours the liquid plane for
      the source
He tastes the salt of the ocean water in order to determine his course

Many years he has fished hoping to find the one who could lead him
      home
A monster of the water with limitations of strength and might unknown

With the ocean still as pane of glass, the fisherman patiently waits
Eyes closed to visualize the breeze that soothes as he contemplates

A song traversing the wind from origins unknown finds his ear
At last his persistence will bear fruit, for the creature he needs is near

With the expertise of lifetimes the fisherman locates the creature's
      voice
A majestic song of angels sung to prepare victims for their coming
      choice

Foam arises from below, near the boat the water swells and crests
Soon eyes of sapphire emerges with diamond scales aligning its chest

Serpentine in appearance the creature towers into the endless sky
Its ivory body seems as if pale moon had descended from on high

Great fins plunge deep into the ocean creating waves like mighty walls
This beast has surely tread among the deep mysterious and unknown
    halls

Without a moment of hesitance, the fisherman leaps toward his prey
Casting line to hook into scale to prevent his catch from getting away

And as destinies become entwined, they dive to reach a place of long
    ago
After great descent they see the glow of Atlantis, the ancient city lost
    deep below

Mind's Freedom

A knight with towel cape and driftwood sword

Slaying monsters hidden within the wind

With fierce battle cry traveling along the coast

Until reaching his liege, the king by the sea

The King hard at work mending muddied walls

From invaders attacking wave after wave

Pulling into the ocean the kingdom he built

He sends word to passing sailor with urgent plea

Hearing the call, the sailor makes for shore

Steering inflatable craft through dangerous waters

With knight and king, she defends battered castle

Until each child is called from the land of make believe

Author Notes: It's fascinating to see kid's use their imagination. It doesn't matter where they are or what objects are around to use, kids will create some sort of fantasy world to keep themselves occupied. People say that kids are indoors too much and are more and more inactive every day, well here's a thought, go outside with them. Kids learn by example and I guarantee if you start playing make believe with them once in a while eventually they will pass up the video games and latest toys just for a chance to play with the box the fridge came in.

My quiet place

Present

With the slumber of the night
Comes the waking of the day
And life begins to emerge from every fleeing shadow
First one by one, then in waves of excitement
Billions of beings live with individual identities
Yet all connected by the fabric of the earth

Inspired to aspire towards success and wealth
Taught that money makes the world go round
Many spend too much time in the future
And overlook the joys of the present
Believing in the happiness to come
Without realizing that joy already surrounds them

Many living ignorant to the beauty of now
I pray they learn to take a moment
To feel the wind so warm and calm upon the skin
To witness the pink hues of light seen throughout the clouds
Like a painting, so still yet full of life
Leaving an imprint in the minds of beholders

To watch the trees reach tall and drink the final rays of light
Taking their fill to last them through the time of darkness
To hear the wind playfully blow through the leaves
And experience the melody of their lullaby sung for all to hear
To smell the perfume of nature filling the ebony sky
The sweet scent of pine and maple, hickory and oak

And as the sun begins to fade, the beauty does not cease
While the moon begins to rise into the black
New life is given birth to continue the circle of life

Search for light

During frostbitten night with ivory moon suspended
Bodies gravitate to each other keeping heat collected
Waiting for droplets of light to announce the dark has ended
Soon one from the crowd will be willingly selected

Chosen to venture into the thick sombre night
To discover why the sun has decided to forever sleep
Chosen to find the alcove hiding the radiant light
And explain to the star that their hearts constantly weep

With iron will the soul sets out into shadow and dust
To find the essence of day amongst the devouring black
Without direction or guidance, he must resolve to trust
Trust that his heart will keep him on the beaten track

Sliver of sunrise on the horizon marks the course
Navigating the void alone, the embodiment of brave
All is worth it when stepping into warmth of the source
And come to the revelation that he emerges from a cave

Author Notes: Anyone that has read the allegory of the cave by Plato can clearly see where I got the inspiration for this poem. After reading Plato's cave in philosophy I was struck by how powerful the use of imagery can be. Instead of plainly explaining your entire theory on a subject you can instead paint a picture of words for the reader to create their own truths. The conclusions that the readers come up with may not be what you originally intended but that is the beauty of it. A thousand people can look at the same picture and get a thousand different things. The uniqueness of the human mind is what makes poetry and the use of images so interesting.

The Secret Garden:

The lush thick moss
Cover the stone
That marks the edge
Of the ancient grove

Where birds lay their heads
And the wildflowers grow
In crimson, violets
And of mystic mauves

The origin of beauty
Comes from this place
Where the sun chooses
To meet with the earth

The angels come down
To sing in the garden
To gaze upon them
Would fill you with mirth

Many have searched
For this garden of joy
Longing to experience
The purity of this place

But to no avail
Do they find what they seek
For they don't understand
The meaning of grace

They can seek the earth
For the entrance of Eden
But will come to understand
That the gate is not without

But in the hearts
Of each and every person
Who looks within
In faith and not doubt

And when found the gate
To the garden of worship
Gaining admission
Is not a monetary toll

All that is needed
When you reach the entrance
Is a pure heart
And a connected soul

The Puzzle

Empty the box, clear the table
Check the clock, ensure surface stable

Surround with chairs, pull in tight
Prepare to stare, bring in brighter light

Begin with border, work your way in
Proceed with order, lest the puzzle may win

Portraits of the sky, mountains and the ocean
Beauty none can deny, caught in still motion

Though a single entity, each piece unique
Similar to humanity, a heavenly technique

Whether children by campfire or castle upon hill
Continue when you tire, to show strength of will

After all pieces laid, and result is viewed
Your heart is weighed, changed is your mood

For in the middle, despite all that's been done
Stands the riddle, of the only missing one

Author Notes: There is a tradition in our house that no matter what size the puzzle or how many people where involved in its putting together, my mom gets to place the last piece. Not sure where it started but it has gotten to the point that even my 7 year old nephew knows that rules and while making a little 50 piece puzzle at our house, he stopped at the end and brought the puzzle to my mother with the last piece for her to put in. But every once in a while you always get the puzzle that is unable to be completed due to that one missing piece that might have been stuck to someone's sock or sucked up the vacuum. What do you do in that situation? Well read the next poem to find out, unless you are reading out of order and you read that one first in which case you already know what happens.

The Missing Piece

You sit and stare, eyes on that spot
A piece should sit there, but instead there is naught

You search the ground, and check the chairs
Seeking as a hound, to ease your cares

You look forever, but to no avail
The piece is clever, at making you fail

You stop trying to find, return to your seat
But you're in a bind, you feel incomplete

You sit and think, mulling the choices
Patience at the brink, quieting inner voices

Before sanity lost, you grab nearby bowl
Worrying not the cost, use it to cover the hole

Though it functions, the truth hidden away
Your mind at a junction, unable to keep it that way

So again you reflect, sweeping the bowl aside
To attain desired effect, without having to hide

After long thought, lightning strikes your brain
Scissors be sought, to make the piece again

With pen and paper, you copy the shape
Cut it then and there, make it stay with tape

But it's easy to point out; your piece is not the same
Removing with a pout, to spare you the shame

In a puzzle so great, why is one piece so vital?
Compared to the pieces that wait, it has no higher title

Regardless of the reason, you feel you're through
Until the committer of treason, is found hiding in plain view

Overwhelmed with glee, the piece is yours to claim
Placing it where it should be, for the missing piece is your name

Author Notes: This is the first continuation poem that I have written which I am starting to do more of. After writing "The Puzzle" I was originally going to leave it at just that, but then I thought how much I hate cliff hangers so I decided to give some closure, if not for anyone else then myself. I didn't want to put the two poems together as one piece because I felt they stand well enough on their own and I liked the fact that I kept the style the same in both poems, just to give them that extra connection.

Come take my hand
To explore beauty uncharted
A journey to the sky
Where the heavens have parted

Where we are welcome
To play with the stars
As children do with fireflies
To catch them in glass jars

Making lamps of the earth
To guide us as we dream
We test the limits of imagination
We push to break the seams

Making the worlds of night and day
One and the very same
A place of joyous harmony
So our children know why we came

Winter Times

Cold and crisp, the air visible
Breathe in; hold winter in your lung
Become as one with the season
Take cue from those with minds so young

Fresh field of snow untouched by man
A canvas to the painter's heart
Be architects of imagination
A land with frozen works of art

Take to the hills with boards and sleds
Ships to carve through frosty ocean
Travelers of the silent waves
Rocky waters in still motion

Make way to icy fortress built
Defend against the flurry sent
With balls of snow and ice and slush
Fight until your fever spent

Then lay in snow with skyward eyes
Clear your mind of stressful things
Dream of endless sun filled days
While spreading arms as angel's wings

Embrace all that has been given
Make the most of each circumstance
Let's remember our inner child
Before we forever miss our chance

Author Notes: I'm like a big kid when it comes to winter. I live in Canada so I figure might as well make the best of all the snow we get. I use to complain when the colder months came around and couldn't wait for summertime but I realized to enjoy what I have for as long as I have it. Sometimes we wait in life for the perfect moment and it never comes around. I would rather live a life full of great moments never knowing what a "perfect" moment feels like, then a life of 1 perfect moment while I spend the rest of it waiting.

Chapter 5: Faith

At the Cross

The five thousand fed
Those raised from the dead
For them he paid the cost
But they were distant at the cross

The possessed that were freed
Those provided their need
They thanked him on that day
But on the cross where were they?

The lost in whom he sought
The multitudes that were taught
They chose to praise his name
But at Calvary they never came

In the end as Jesus hung
Aching body, gasping lung
Was a criminal nearing death
That learned before final breath

That Jesus is truly royalty
The lion worthy of loyalty
Not by miracles performed
Or the way that he was born

But by being at the cross
On the day when all seemed lost
To witness the willing sacrifice
Choose to pay the ultimate price

Author notes: How many of us have friends that are only our friends as long as we give them stuff or agree with them, but the second things get a little rocky or something might not got their way all of a sudden it's like they never knew you. I have to admit that I have treated Jesus like this at times, giving him glory and praise as long as life is good, but as soon as things get shaky he is the first one I blame for my misfortunes. We shouldn't worship Jesus solely on what he does for us but instead for whom he is.

Creation

To plant a seed,
A tree will grow
To dig a trench,
A river will flow

To strike a match,
A fire will form
To light a fuse
Mountains are torn

To dig a well
A spring will rise
To build a mill
We harness the skies

To place a rod
Lightning directed
To lay a panel
The sun collected

We do all this
For we are debated
That God's awesome power
Is beyond we created

So some choose to pursue
The pathway of creation
To become a god
To rule over the nation

Soon they will learn
This is not a game
And they will witness
The Lion of Judah untamed

For with the stamp of his feet
Land became known
The shedding of his tears
Oceans began to foam

The strike of his fist
Valleys started to form
The clap of his hands
Called forth the storm

With one single thought
The sun began to burn
And with another
The seasons started to turn

The moulding of dirt
Created husband and wife
The exhale of his breath
Used to stimulate life

But beyond his power
Something greater exists
A concept unattainable
Despite how we persist

The notion of forgiveness
Of unconditional love
The power that compelled
Jesus' descent from above

Cycle

As a river, ever constant flow
Charged to reach those I know
Every turn and bend to reach forgotten friend
I pray they choose to follow

To embrace a life of movement and change
The risk of not knowing
Your world rearranged
Pursue this course
So this river may grow
As we gain momentum to reach our goal
May this river continue to flow

With new addition
The current gains speed
Swelling and spreading
Searching those in need
Join the surge as we push ahead
Soon we'll be where many tread

Now our purpose within our sight
We flow into great and mighty ocean
The population kept within the night
Here we'll flow creating motion
Spreading a simple message of light
Hopefully they'll grasp the notion

I will flow and continue to feed
Giving everything I have in me
But soon I fear that I'll run dry
 I need to find replenished supply

So to the sky I will ascend
Empty, I ask you fill my cup
Replenish all that is within
My strength and fervour again rise up
Take me, transform me and choose to send
So for you I may flow like a river again

Author Notes: When I was writing this poem I was coming out of a writing block that I had for a few weeks. With everything that I was writing I wasn't really putting anything back in my head to recharge the batteries. I wasn't reading poetry or even living life just to be inspired; I tried to force rhymes but then when I looked back at them I was like blegh, who wrote that? It's important that no matter what you do, you must find that place of renewal that will allow you to keep on keeping on.

Earth Song

From the heavens do the winds blow
Gently whistling through children's hair
Bringing forth the rain and the snow
Washing away the pain and despair

The tremor of the bass from far beneath
Shakes the earth to its very core
Expanding farther than imagination can reach
Bringing forth the desire to explore

The steady trickle of the bubbling brook
Soothes the ache that comes from life
Returning to us which life once took
Melodies reminiscent of the days without strife

The thundering roar of the raging fire
Those able to control its power are rare
Always burning intense without tire
Dangerous when handled without care

The world is his grand stage
And the elements are his band
If you were to ask who he is
He simply responds "I Am the I Am"

Forgiven

I live amongst the lions
But no harm befalls my head
If it weren't for my God's shelter
Long ago would I be dead
With him by my side
There is no path I fear to tread
As long as I remember in my heart
That none would compare in his stead

When I turn away from God
The world closes in and clutches tight
The overwhelming temptations
Completely blots out the light
I am told that I am fine
But I know I have lost my sight
I try to escape their grasp
But by myself I lack the might
My only condolence during this time
That pushes me to fight
Is that in the darkest of hours
Is when hope shines most bright

I humbly return to God
The shame too much to bear
I fall unto my knees
Asking forgiveness in my prayer
He looks into my heart
To judge all he finds there
He begins to smile
Lifting me with most gentle care

He speaks to me
A voice filled with power and affection
"When under attack
I will be your protection
The road will be tough
But through reflection
Earnestly seek me out
Choose to create the connection
If this is what you want
I will gladly show you the direction
Remember my son
And the story of his resurrection"

Author Notes: Life is difficult and many times we fall short of the glory of God, it is only through his forgiveness that we live. No matter what you have done you are never far from God as long as you seek him.

Harvest

Feel the earth, feel desperate yearn

To be cultivated and in turn

Give life to harvest carefully grown

To witness dust turn into bone

But touch cold soil, realize the toil

Much work is needed

Before the Gatherer is known

Wait not for frost, to claim the lost

Seeds be planted

Until the last are sown

Soon barren ground,

Will creek and sound

New life will peak from gentle mound

Be prepared, as it's declared

A new harvest to the world is found

Author Notes: This poem was actually a dream I had not too long ago. Usually I forget my dreams by the time I wake up but this one was just as vivid even more so when I recalled it. Even now, every time I read it the same pictures pop into my head as if i was dreaming all over again.

Immaculate

Upon our birth
We are given
A tablet pure and strong
A blank slate
To record our deeds
Whether they be right or wrong

The good written
With steady hand
Clear, ordered and plain
But our sins
Carelessly printed
Mar our life with blemish and stain

And as we live
The stone is etched
Permanent, firm and true
Despite our attempt
To suppress and forget
It can never be made anew

Until we meet
The son of God
Powerful, loving and wise
And in our hearts
Choose to trust
In him and not in lies

He'll reach out
And take our slate
Broken, beaten and torn
Wash with blood
So we may know
A tablet given to the reborn

Author notes: I first thought of the 10 commandments that were written on stone tablets when writing this. From there I imagined what it would be like if all of our resumes and personal documents were put on stone slabs for everyone to see. Nowadays a simple click of the mouse and strike of the key can change who we are and what we have done but obviously the change is superficial. I think if everything was set in stone we wouldn't believe we could lie so easily to those around us and perhaps choose to live a better life.

The Secret Garden

Immersed

Have you ever taken the time to examine your soul?
To look past the shields that guards your core
Have you ever wondered about life's true goal?
Have you ever in your heart wanted for more

These desires are expected if you just look around
With the pain, sickness and death, this land is cursed
How do you escape the pain, do you hide underground?
The only answer my friend, is to become immersed

Take heed to the twelve who followed our Lord
Those who were changed by delving into His life
Each one selected to be separate from the horde
Each one to walk the road of love, joy and strife

From many paths of life they were found and called
To experience something far greater than earth
Lifted from their feet no longer needing to crawl
For soon each would know the meaning of rebirth

This gift is not given for simply knowing His name
But by living as disciples who walk daily at His side
Submerging in His teachings, to feed the flame
To respect and remember the reasons why he died

Then dedicate your lives to his wisdom and ways
To learn and comprehend his word verse by verse
You will know fulfillment for the rest of your days
As you continue to become more and more immersed

Masterpiece

Fresh canvas stretched over the wooden frame
Candle light cascades shadows upon the cloth
Delicately the painter sets the fabric on the stand
To begin his masterpiece, the painting without a name

Staring at the canvas, he envisions the work of art
Images of women and flowers dance through his mind
But despite the many inspirations, none seem to help
So he closes his eyes to see the painting in his heart

Taking brush and palette in hand, his arms finally whole
Covering bristles in paint he makes for the first stroke
At first he hesitates unable to mar the purity of the cloth
But he pushes on knowing this painting will touch the soul

Streaks of indescribable colours cover the entire page
Shades of green embodying the beauty of nature
Pools of blue capturing the strength of the ocean
The painter's arm free like a bird released from its cage

After six days of labour his masterpiece is given birth
The painter smiles as he inspects his work of art
An image so alive that it seems almost real
For the painting without a name is one of Earth

Author Notes: One of the earliest poems I have written that is included in this book, the masterpiece is one of my twist ending poems that I enjoy so much. I think we all love twists and turns in writing and movies because anything that catches us off guard is new and exciting. We like not knowing what will happen next and the excitement of discovery takes over. Can you picture a world where we knew everything that was going to happen in the world for your entire life? That would be horribly boring, especially if you could do nothing to change it.

My Desire

It's my desire that my name be arrayed
With shimmering text upon the ebony page
Burnt into the black beyond the sun
Resting beyond the reach of the future horizon
Speaking the language of the keepers of time
The sun and moon will view it and know that it is mine
And in the night with the darkness engulfing
I want people to raise their heads so their eyes can react to the glow
To see my name there amongst the stars and know
That I am not content to live behind the stage, to be kept in the cold
        by another's shadow
I want to be included with great minds like, Martin Luther, Mark Twain
        and Edgar Allan Poe.
There's a knocking at the door, leave it closed its only a raven
Focus on these words and realize what I am craving
I want to be like a brand
When you hear of nike, you think sports attire
When you hear of powerade, you think energy
When you hear of walmart, you think the place I can get anything from
        a tire to a baby
In suit I want people to think when they hear my name that maybe just
        maybe...they will think of excellence
But what I didn't realize in my dreams of popularity
In my pursuit of happiness which focused on how others viewed me
All my planning to propel my name through glory
What about he who wrote my story
I mean who am I?
What is my claim to fame that gives people the reason to want to know
        my name?
As a matter of fact what is anyone's claim?
Oh he plays sports well
Or she's been in a bunch of great movies

Her voice is entrancing or his songs are filled with sick rhymes
What about being the dissecting line in time
To be the man who can walk on oceans
And then reach down and turn that water to wine
The person who raises the dead
Who's known as our daily bread?
Who 2000 years ago hung on a cross and bled
Jesus, The one who has done more than all of us combined
Came not for parties, money or to experience the status of celebrity
But to share a truth of deepness and longevity
The deepest I can get is to write with parchment and quiver
But the ink that Jesus used, it makes me shiver
He wrote with actions and sacrifice
Even as he lay on the cross while soldiers below cast dice
I can only imagine as his blood spilled forth on the stones
Those red rivers becoming words along the lines
Saying flesh of my flesh and bone of my bone
For we are his children and because of that he came to atone
By descending from his throne
To make it known
That in the middle of chaos or the quiet of silence we are not alone
I think about his humility
It's made me re-evaluate my priority
So what if my name is forgotten
If I can help at least one soul to God's only begotten
Who cares about fame or recognition?
If I can follow the great commission
To this new focus I pray I'll never tire
To follow Jesus is now my one and only desire

Author Notes: I performed this piece as my first crack at spoken word. Although written poetry and spoken word are pretty much the same thing, I feel spoken word is more how you present the poem. It is more of a performance that is personal in terms of style and portrayal but when you look at spoken word on paper like this, it can be read like most other poems. Depending on how you read a poem or how you hear it can also affect what you get out of it which is fascinating to me.

Remembrance:

In a world so incomplete
There's a miraculous feat
We show who we really are
When we try to make some sense
Of a world that is so tense
Looking for answers on earth
Trying to prove our own worth
Instead of looking above
For answers given in love
Demonstrated by the cross
And everything that it caused
The days of old long forgot
The price at which we were bought
Not by any coins of gold
But by blood whose worth's untold
And the loving sacrifice
That was used to pay the price
With the piercing of the lance
We received another chance
So we may spread his story
And give him all the glory

The Powers of Words

Always Allowing Antagonists an Amount of Animosity against Angry
    Actions

Blissfully Banking Blessings behind Bountiful Bushes Bursting with
    Berries

Characters Carefully Contemplating Clever Concoctions To Catch
    Criminals

Desperately Demanding Detours Ditching Destinations to Denial

Each Example Endangering Earth's Eloquence Elaborately Exiled

Falling Far From Fighting, Furthering Fate's Frustration

Gladly Giving Great Gifts of Gratitude Gathered Gently from God

Hard Hearts Healed Happily Having Hope Heaped on High

Injustice is Irresponsible Individuals Indulging in Illegal Itineraries

Jesus (let's face it, that's all that needs to be said)

Author Notes: alliterations are fun because no matter what you say it sounds cool, or at least I think so. It's surprising that the English language offers so many words that give the opportunity to write a poem like this where each sentence makes sense on its own but also comes together to push a single point across. I want to challenge people to try to come up with the longest alliteration that makes sense and share it with your friends just to see their reaction.

The Real Battle

When we look outside...
People dying, people crying
It's a scene we see everyday
From dawn till dusk, people turning others to dust
Trying to pave a way
For the children of tomorrow but from all this sorrow
They'll be the ones who pay
How to change our direction to ensure the next generation
Has a place to play?

We have to look within...
The real battle isn't with someone else but within ourselves
In the shadows of our mind
It's not fought with AKs or switchblades
But weapons far harder to find
The enemy is false right down to his pulse
In his web he wants us to bind
He is unseen, always been
A master at being deceptively kind

We must prepare...
He will always pretend to be your closest friend
Saying to please you is all he yearns
But once you turn around, he'll kick you to the ground
And laugh as your soul begins to burn
So don't give him the chance, to thrust his lance
Instead grab the armour of God and learn
The ways of the light, so you can finally fight
The real battle and make things start to turn

The Wrestler

Conscience awakening to the pitch black
Strangers nearby muttering incoherent thought
Your mind wanders your body slack
As you try to listen to what's being taught

But before your mind can grasp the situation
A great shove pushes you through dark curtains
As you are welcomed by a crowd of the nation
To feel happiness or fear, you are not certain

A path stretches to a ring in the distance
The crowd's thunderous cheering urging you ahead
Your feet slide forward despite your resistance
Understanding diminishing each step you tread

Stepping into the ring, you see the opposition
Two men of indomitable size and standing
Your deepest fears coming into fruition
You feel the circumstances far too demanding

Before you can challenge the fairness of the fight
The bell is rung and the onslaught begins
Instantly overcome by the adversary's might
Your only thought is survival, let alone to win

Your body is pummelled with metal and fist
Bruised and beaten is your flesh and mind
All your logic and reason now lost to the mist
A friendly face is what you wish to find

You see them there watching the entire bout
Your friends cheering you on from the side
You look into their eyes, PLEASE HELP!!! You shout
 But they refuse saying, this is all we can provide

Your foe grows tired and halts his attack
You try to get to your feet and run away
But he tags his partner to continue in his track
Another round of torment to your dismay

With chairs and ladders received from the crowd
He delivers each hit with no glimpse of remorse
All the while the arena cheers deafeningly loud
Desperate cries for escape turns your throat hoarse

Soon struggling is futile, the end approaching
Your mind thankful that the pin-count will arrive
1...you can feel the entire arena encroaching
2...but your heart feels that something is very alive

In your corner you see a man screaming your name
Why have you not noticed him before?
He has always been there, since the moment you came
Telling you to trust in him to even the score

And with strength unknown, you break the pin
Running to him, your safety no longer a bother
Placing your life in his hands, knowing he will win
For no child is ever neglected from this loving father

Unite

Timeless Anchor

At times it seems that life is a mess

Everything jumbled, the ease and the stress

Jam packed days with sleep cut short

Time lost as we walk confusion's court

The pressure comes upon us like continuous tide

We get pulled further in with every stride

Until we are lost, alone in the sea

Alone to wonder how it all came to be

But in the ocean, in the midst of it all

Stands the precious cross, strong and tall

An anchor to hold on to until the waters recede

The cross to remain for as long as we need

Transformation

We begin our lives as untouched ore
Without a known purpose of our own
Hard and cold to the very core
Waiting for the one able to atone

And when he chooses to arrive
Leaving his footprints in the sand
He will take a look at all of our lives
And reach out with once pierced hands

Leaning towards each daughter and son
He grabs us and holds us to his heart
Gently reaching out for us one by one
He takes us to his shop in order to start

Setting us down as he takes a seat
The kiln burns with flames of salvation
We're placed inside and purified by the heat
Malleable are we, to be a new creation

And through our time amongst the ember
Cold and callous hearts are melted away
As our minds begin to remember
What he did on that fateful day

He takes from the furnace with hands bare
And sets us not in casts but on his table
Allowing his children to form as they care
Offering his guidance to keep us stable

From the cold stones that we once were
We were changed by his hands anew
To become creations both precious and pure
Objects of his mercy and love true

He lets us go into the world to teach
And it seems as if his job is done
But instead he makes his way to the beach
And picks up new stones one by one

Author Notes: I have banned my cousin Danny from reading this poem as every time he chooses to do so he puts on some ridiculous accent despite my pleas. That being said I still like the poem because I am a big fan towards the concept of rebirth and renewal. The idea that the end is the beginning has always intrigued me so I guess instead of saying good bye and thanks for reading my poems, I will say thanks and start looking out for the next book.